Real-Life Queens

Karen Latchana Kenney

BUMBA BOOKS™

LERNER PUBLICATIONS ◆ MINNEAPOLIS

Note to Educators

Throughout this book, you'll find critical-thinking questions. These can be used to engage young readers in thinking critically about the topic and in using the text and photos to do so.

Copyright © 2020 by Lerner Publishing Group, Inc.

All rights reserved. International copyright secured. No part of this book may be reproduced, stored in a retrieval system, or transmitted in any form or by any means—electronic, mechanical, photocopying, recording, or otherwise—without the prior written permission of Lerner Publishing Group, Inc., except for the inclusion of brief quotations in an acknowledged review.

Lerner Publications Company
An imprint of Lerner Publishing Group, Inc.
241 First Avenue North
Minneapolis, MN 55401 USA

For reading levels and more information, look up this title at www.lernerbooks.com.

Main body text set in Helvetica Textbook Com Roman 23/49.
Typeface provided by Linotype AG.

Library of Congress Cataloging-in-Publication Data

Names: Kenney, Karen Latchana, author.
Title: Real-life queens / Karen Latchana Kenney.
Description: Minneapolis, Minnesota : Lerner Publications, [2019] | Series: Bumba Books — Real-life royalty | Includes bibliographical references and index. | Audience: Grades K–3. | Audience: Ages 4–7.
Identifiers: LCCN 2018049346 (print) | LCCN 2018058296 (ebook) | ISBN 9781541561342 (eb pdf) | ISBN 9781541557314 (lb : alk. paper) | ISBN 9781541573598 (pb : alk. paper)
Subjects: LCSH: Queens—Juvenile literature.
Classification: LCC D107.3 (ebook) | LCC D107.3 .K46 2019 (print) | DDC 920.72—dc23

LC record available at https://lccn.loc.gov/2018049346

Manufactured in the United States of America
1-46146-45751-3/13/2019

Table of Contents

Let's Meet a Queen! **4**

Life as a Queen **22**

Picture Glossary **23**

Read More **24**

Index **24**

Let's Meet a Queen!

It's Queen Elizabeth's birthday!

She celebrates.

She waves to crowds.

Queen Elizabeth from the United Kingdom

Queen Elizabeth is the head of the British royal family. Her father was the king. Her son Charles is next in line to be king.

Queen Elizabeth meets with her country's leaders.

She listens to them.

She gives them advice.

Some queens are not born in royal families.

They marry a king.

Queen Rania married King Abdullah.

Queens dress up for special events.

A queen sometimes wears a crown and gown.

Why might a queen wear a crown?

Queen Sonja from Norway

Queen Elizabeth from the United Kingdom

13

Queen Jetsun Pema from Bhutan

14

A queen makes royal visits.

Queen Jetsun Pema visits another country.

She meets the country's leaders and people.

Why might a queen visit another country?

A queen works with charities.

She helps her people.

Queen Silvia from Sweden

Leaders visit a queen's country.

She spends time with them.

Queen Margrethe has a banquet for her visitors.

A queen is an important leader. She serves her country in many ways.

Queen Mathilde from Belgium

21

Picture Glossary

banquet: a big dinner to honor important people

celebrates: does something special to honor an important day

charities: groups that come together to help people

gown: a formal dress worn for special events

Read More

Hansen, Grace. *Queen Elizabeth II: The World's Longest-Reigning Monarch.* Minneapolis: Abdo Kids, 2018.

Kenney, Karen Latchana. *Real-Life Kings.* Minneapolis: Lerner Publications, 2020.

Kenney, Karen Latchana. *Real-Life Princesses.* Minneapolis: Lerner Publications, 2020.

Index

banquet, 19

crown, 12

Elizabeth (queen), 4, 7, 8

king, 7, 11

visits, 15, 19

Photo Credits

Image credits: Chris Jackson/Getty Images, pp. 5, 17, 23 (top right), 23 (bottom left); Alberto Pezzali/NurPhoto/Getty Images, p. 6; Matt Dunham/AFP/Getty Images, p. 9; Mandel Ngan/AFP/Getty Images, p. 10; Tim Graham Picture Library/Getty Images, pp. 13; 23 (bottom right); Yoshikazu Tsuno/AFP/Getty Images, p. 14; Philip Reynaers/Photonews/Getty Images, pp. 18, 23 (top left); Didier Lebrun/Photo News/Getty Images, p. 21; John Stillwell/PA Images/Getty Images, p. 22 (gown); Haakon Mosvold Larsen/AFP/Getty Images, p. 22 (sash); Julian Stratenschulte/picture alliance/Getty Images, p. 22 (crown); Pascal Le Segretain/Getty Images, p. 22 (banquet).

Cover: Mark Cuthbert/UK Press/Getty Images.